Adapted from *The Jungle Book* and *The Second Jungle Book* by Rudyard Kipling
Retold by Sarah Powell
Illustrated by Federica Frenna

STUDIO
PRESS

© 2018 Studio Press

Edited by Gemma Cooper • Designed by Claire Munday
Consultant John Walker, the Kipling Society
www.kiplingsociety.co.uk

Printed and bound in China, 0240917
2 4 6 8 10 9 7 5 3 1

Studio Press
An imprint of Kings Road Publishing
Part of Bonnier Publishing
The Plaza, 535 King's Road,
London, SW10 0SZ
www.studiopressbooks.co.uk
www.bonnierpublishing.co.uk

The Jungle Book

A Search & Find Book

Illustrated by Federica Frenna
Original story by Rudyard Kipling • Retold by Sarah Powell

With an introduction by John Walker, the Kipling Society

Rudyard Kipling
1865–1936

One of the most widely known, quoted and admired writers in English is Joseph Rudyard Kipling. He was born in Mumbai, India, and lived there with his parents until he was brought to England at the age of five, along with his three-year old sister, to avoid tropical illnesses and to start school.

At first, he lived in a foster home but was desperately unhappy. After four years at a boarding school in Southsea, Rudyard returned to India at the age of sixteen to work as a journalist. He had already begun writing short stories and poetry, and was quickly recognised as a new and exciting talent. After travelling back to England in 1889, he became an overnight sensation in the eyes of other writers, critics and the general public. He married and moved to the United States of America to be near his new wife's family in Vermont. There he wrote the two *Jungle Books* and *Captains Courageous*, and began telling many of the tales from *Just So Stories* to his two daughters. His reputation grew quickly from early critical success into international celebrity.

In 1907, he was awarded the Nobel Prize in Literature. Kipling remains the youngest-ever English recipient of the prize. He went on to publish the wonderful *Puck* stories, in addition to *Just So Stories* and *Kim*, all of which have remained in print ever since. Having lost his son, John, in the First World War, Kipling worked with the War Graves Commission and continued writing powerful, original and masterful prose and verse until his death. Kipling was buried at Poets' Corner in Westminster Abbey, London.

The Jungle Book
1894

Apart from his poem 'If', Rudyard Kipling is best known for the two *Jungle Books*. Kipling wrote the stories in two books when he was newly married and living in Vermont. His baby daughter, Josephine, was almost certainly in his mind when he wrote them. The stories feature many different jungle animals, from monkeys and jackals to an old cobra, a family of wolves, and a mongoose called Rikki-Tikki-Tavi. Scattered throughout these tales are the adventures of a human child called Mowgli (pronounced "Maow-glee") who is separated from his parents as a young boy and lives in the jungle with his animal family and friends.

Whenever people retell the stories, whether as a cartoon or a film, there will always be a protective and strict black panther, a terrifying man-eating tiger, and a loving, old brown bear. We imagine the huge and powerful python, Kaa, the rampaging wild dogs, the thieving monkeys, and the stately, wise elephants. But always at the centre of each retelling is the young orphan Mowgli.

Featuring some illustrations by Rudyard's father, John Lockwood, *The Jungle Book* was published in 1894 and *The Second Jungle Book* in 1895. Both books quickly became worldwide best sellers, and have been translated into dozens of languages. Although the stories were written over 120 years ago, they remain in print and loved by readers to this day.

John Walker, the Kipling Society

Meet the Characters

There is a marvellous world of characters waiting to be discovered on the search and find pages, from Mowgli and his adopted wolf family to Baloo the bear, Bagheera the panther and Shere Khan the tiger.

MOWGLI, A BOY

"And he grew, and grew strong as a boy must grow who does not know that he is learning any lessons, and who has nothing in the world to think of except things to eat."

BALOO, A BEAR

"As the creeper that girdles the tree trunk, the Law runneth forward and back – for the strength of the pack is the wolf, and the strength of the wolf is the pack."

BAGHEERA, A PANTHER

AKELA, A WOLF

A FAMILY OF WOLVES

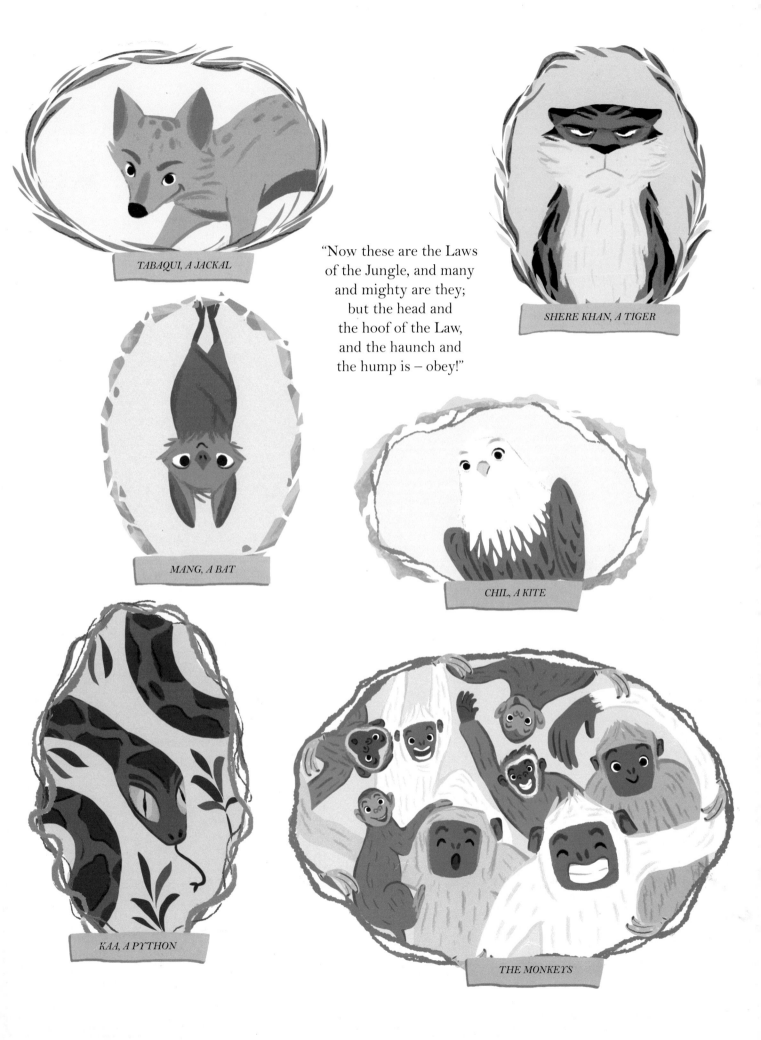

TABAQUI, A JACKAL

SHERE KHAN, A TIGER

"Now these are the Laws of the Jungle, and many and mighty are they; but the head and the hoof of the Law, and the haunch and the hump is – obey!"

MANG, A BAT

CHIL, A KITE

KAA, A PYTHON

THE MONKEYS

The Attack of Shere Khan

In which …

A woodcutter family makes camp at night,
Shere Khan the tiger watches and waits,
He attacks the camp with a roar,
Mischievous Tabaqui scavenges for food,
The woodcutter scares both away with fire,
Young Mowgli escapes, but becomes lost,
A wolf family discovers him, and
Mother Wolf adopts Mowgli as her cub.

Search and find:

A SCARED
MOWGLI

FOUR WOODEN
STOOLS

A STALKING
TABAQUI

A SPILLED
COOKING POT

A ROARING
SHERE KHAN

A WOODCUTTER'S
AXE

A FRIGHTENED
MOTHER

A BURNING
TORCH

AN OBSERVING
WOLF

EIGHT NAUGHTY
MONKEYS

The Wolf Council

At which ...

Mowgli is presented to the wolf pack,
The wolves wonder who will guard him,
Shere Khan roars that the boy is his,
Bagheera vows to protect Mowgli,
Baloo offers to teach him the jungle laws,
Akela orders Shere Khan to go,
Shere Khan leaves, promising revenge, and,
Mowgli goes home with his new family.

Search and find:

*A PLAYFUL
MOWGLI*

*A CONCERNED
FATHER WOLF*

*A LISTENING
AKELA*

*FOUR YOUNG
WOLF CUBS*

*A THOUGHTFUL
BAGHEERA*

*A CURIOUS
MONKEY*

*A WATCHING
BALOO*

*AN AMUSED
TABAQUI*

*A PROTECTIVE
MOTHER WOLF*

*AN ANGRY
SHERE KHAN*

The Man-cub, Mowgli

In which …

Mowgli plays with the wolf pack,
His wolf mother teaches him to howl,
His wolf father teaches him to hunt,
His wolf brother teaches him to swim,
His wolf sister teaches him to leap,
He runs with the wolf pack every day,
Mowgli grows big and strong, and
Shere Khan waits patiently.

Search and find:

A SWIMMING MOWGLI

A SPLASHING BROTHER WOLF

A SLEEPING BAGHEERA

A LEAPING SISTER WOLF

A GREEDY BALOO

A PROWLING SHERE KHAN

A HOWLING MOTHER WOLF

A TRACKING TABAQUI

A HUNTING FATHER WOLF

TWO CHEEKY MONKEYS

The Laws of the Jungle

In which …

Baloo teaches Mowgli the jungle laws,
He learns to talk with the animals,
Snakes slither by to hiss with him,
Birds swoop in to sing with him,
Bagheera shows Mowgli how to climb,
He becomes exhausted from his lessons,
Monkeys watch from behind the trees, and
Bagheera guards Mowgli as he sleeps.

Search and find:

*A CHATTING
MOWGLI*

*FIVE SPYING
MONKEYS*

*A SINGING
PARAKEET*

*A NEST OF
HONEYBEES*

*AN AMUSED
BAGHEERA*

*A SPYING
TABAQUI*

*FOUR GREEN
FROGS*

*A WATCHING
CHIL*

*A HISSING
SNAKE*

*A SWARM OF
BUTTERFLIES*

The Monkey Thieves

In which …

The monkeys steal Mowgli,
He is swung through the trees,
Bagheera chases but cannot keep up,
The monkeys quickly swing away,
Chil the kite tries to help,
Baloo and Bagheera wonder what to do,
A rescue plan is made, and
They decide to visit Kaa, the snake.

Search and find:

*A KIDNAPPED
MOWGLI*

*A SQUAWKING
HORNBILL*

*TWO CHEEKY
MONKEYS*

*TWO BLACK
BEETLES*

*A STRIPY
MONKEY*

*A CHASING
BAGHEERA*

*A LAUGHING
TABAQUI*

*FIVE COLOURFUL
LIZARDS*

*AN INDIAN
CHAMELEON*

*A SOARING
CHIL*

The Giant, Kaa

In which …

Baloo and Bagheera ask for Kaa's help,
Kaa agrees to help save Mowgli,
He knows where the monkeys live,
Mang offers to join the rescue,
Chil helps them find the Cold Lairs,
Bagheera races along the forest floor,
Kaa slithers across the branches, and
Baloo runs as fast as he can.

Search and find:

A LISTENING
KAA

A HELPFUL
MANG

FIVE GOLDEN
FISH

IKKI,
A PORCUPINE

A RAINBOW
BEETLE

JACALA,
A CROCODILE

A CRAWLING
TARANTULA

FERAO,
A WOODPECKER

A RESTING
CHIL

OO,
A TURTLE

The Chaos in the Cold Lairs

In which …

Mowgli discovers he is in the Cold Lairs,
The monkeys all whoop excitedly,
Hundreds come to see the man-cub,
Mowgli explores the crumbling ruins,
The monkeys are noisy and troublesome,
One of the monkeys makes a speech,
The monkeys sing foolish songs, and
Mowgli hopes his friends will rescue him.

Search and find:

*A CONFUSED
MOWGLI*

*A TALKING
MONKEY*

*AN UPSIDE-DOWN
MONKEY*

*A STEALING
MONKEY*

*A STATUESQUE
MONKEY*

*THREE SINGING
MONKEYS*

*A HUNGRY
MONKEY*

*A WATCHING
PARROT*

*A NAUGHTY
MONKEY*

*FIVE BABY
MONKEYS*

The Monkeys Learn a Lesson

In which …

Poor Mowgli is tired and hungry,
The monkeys demand a lesson,
Mowgli tries to teach them to weave,
The monkeys prefer to play,
Mowgli wants to go home,
Kaa slithers into the temple,
Bagheera lurks in the shadows, and
Baloo waits behind the rocks.

Search and find:

*AN UNHAPPY
MOWGLI*

*A HAPPY
MONKEY*

*FIVE MONKEY
STATUES*

*A SPYING
CHIL*

*A WAITING
MANG*

*A HIDING
KAA*

*A CLIMBING
MONKEY*

*A PATIENT
BAGHEERA*

*TWO PAIRS OF
GLASSES*

*A GRUMBLING
BALOO*

The Rescue

In which …

Bagheera pounces like a lightning bolt,
Baloo roars loudly, beating his paws,
Kaa hypnotises the angry monkeys,
Mowgli hides in the python pit,
Hundreds of monkeys flee in terror,
Mowgli climbs on to Baloo's back,
They all escape the Cold Lairs, and
Mowgli hugs his rescuers with relief.

Search and find:

*A FLEEING
MOWGLI*

*A PIT OF
SNAKES*

*A POUNCING
BAGHEERA*

*A RUNNING
BALOO*

*A SCREECHING
CHIL*

*A HYPNOTISED
TABAQUI*

*A FLYING
MANG*

*A FLOCK OF
PARROTS*

*A SWAYING
KAA*

*A SLEEPING
MONKEY*

The Red Flower Thief

In which …

Shere Khan returns ready for revenge,
Only the red flower will protect Mowgli,
Bagheera tells Mowgli he must find it,
Mowgli searches the jungle in vain,
He discovers that the red flower is fire,
Mowgli travels to a nearby village,
He waits until night falls, and
Mowgli steals a pot of fire.

Search and find:

*A CRAWLING
MOWGLI*

*FIVE BURNING
CAMPFIRES*

*A HIDING
BALOO*

*A BUSY
WOODCUTTER*

*A CREEPING
BAGHEERA*

*TWO SPYING
CHILDREN*

*A PROWLING
SHERE KHAN*

*A DANCING
MAN*

*A WATCHING
AKELA*

*A SCHEMING
TABAQUI*

The Attack at Council Rock

In which …

Shere Khan storms the wolf council,
The wolves discover Mowgli is a thief,
Mowgli's wolf family reject him,
He must face the tiger all alone,
Shere Khan pounces to attack,
Mowgli waves the burning torch,
Shere Khan runs away scared, and
Mowgli knows he must leave the jungle.

Search and find:

*AN ANGRY
MOWGLI*

*A FURIOUS
SHERE KHAN*

*A SCARED
BALOO*

*A STOLEN
POT OF FIRE*

*AN ANXIOUS
BAGHEERA*

*A GIGGLING
TABAQUI*

*A DEPARTING
AKELA*

*A SAD
MOTHER WOLF*

*A FLEEING
BROTHER WOLF*

*AN ASHAMED
FATHER WOLF*

The Village and Mowgli

In which …

Mowgli runs away to the village,
A family takes him in,
Mowgli learns about village life,
The wolf pack misses Mowgli,
Mowgli misses his wolf brothers,
Mowgli teaches the villagers to hunt,
Baloo and Bagheera visit in secret, and
Mowgli is given a village job.

Search and find:

*A LEARNING
MOWGLI*

*A WOMAN
FETCHING WATER*

*A CONCERNED
BROTHER WOLF*

*A WATCHING
AKELA*

*A BASKET OF
PAWPAWS*

*A STALKING
SHERE KHAN*

*A BOX OF
NUTS*

*A FORGOTTEN
BOW AND ARROW SET*

*A NECKLACE OF
FLOWERS*

*TWO FISHING
RODS*

The Defeat of Shere Khan

In which …

Shere Khan arrives to attack the village,
Mowgli's wolf family race to the rescue,
Shere Khan runs into a ravine,
Mowgli thinks of a clever plan,
The wolves chase the buffalo,
The buffalo stampede along the ravine,
Shere Khan is swept away, and
Mowgli decides to return to the jungle.

Search and find:

*A SHOUTING
MOWGLI*

*A LEAPING
SISTER WOLF*

*A RUNNING
AKELA*

*A POINTING
VILLAGER*

*A BELLOWING
BALOO*

*A SCARED
TABAQUI*

*A RELIEVED
VILLAGER*

*A DEFEATED
SHERE KHAN*

*A GALLOPING
BABY BUFFALO*

*A SURPRISED
BAGHEERA*

The Return of Mowgli

In which …

Mowgli returns happily to the jungle,
His wolf brothers howl with welcome,
Hathi the elephant toots a greeting,
Chil screeches with glee,
Kaa hisses a hello,
Baloo dances in happiness,
Bagheera quietly purrs, and
Mowgli vows to stay in the jungle forever.

Search and find:

*A HAPPY
MOWGLI*

*A TRUMPETING
HATHI*

*A SLITHERING
KAA*

*TWO KISSING
PARROTS*

*A CONTENTED
BAGHEERA*

*FOUR BABY
WOLF CUBS*

*A HOWLING
BROTHER WOLF*

*A RESTING
AKELA*

*A SWOOPING
CHIL*

*A JOYFUL
BALOO*

THE ATTACK OF SHERE KHAN

THE WOLF COUNCIL

THE MAN-CUB, MOWGLI

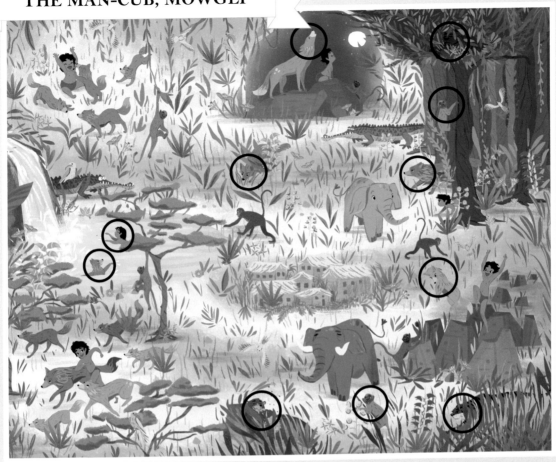

THE LAWS OF THE JUNGLE

THE MONKEY THIEVES

THE GIANT, KAA

THE CHAOS IN THE COLD LAIRS

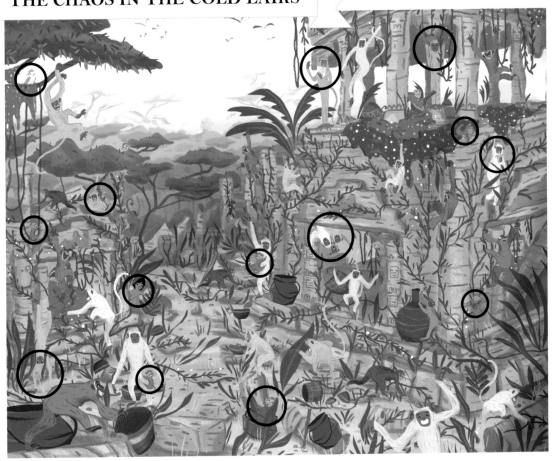

THE MONKEYS LEARN A LESSON

THE RESCUE

THE RED FLOWER THIEF

THE ATTACK AT COUNCIL ROCK

THE VILLAGE AND MOWGLI

THE DEFEAT OF SHERE KHAN

THE RETURN OF MOWGLI